Ancient of Days

50

FAVORITES FOR CHOIR, CONGREGATION, OR ENSEMBLE
USABLE IN MEDLEYS OR INDIVIDUALLY

Compiled and Arranged by

MARTY PARKS

Accompaniment / Solo Edition

Lillenas PUBLISHING COMPANY
Box 419572, Kansas City, MO 64141
www.lillenas.com

MW00700245

Song begins on page 2 in the Choral Edition

LIVING HOPE

includes
Firm Foundation
We Want to See Jesus Lifted High

Medley arranged by Marty Parks

Presentation Suggestions:
FIRM FOUNDATION: Refrain; Verse 1, D.S.; Refrain; Verse 2, D.S.; Refrain, Coda and medley ending
WE WANT TO SEE JESUS LIFTED HIGH: As written, with repeats

Firm Foundation

Words and Music by
NANCY GORDON
and JAMIE HARVILL
Arranged by Marty Parks

We Want to See Jesus Lifted High

Words and Music by
DOUG HORLEY
Arranged by Marty Parks

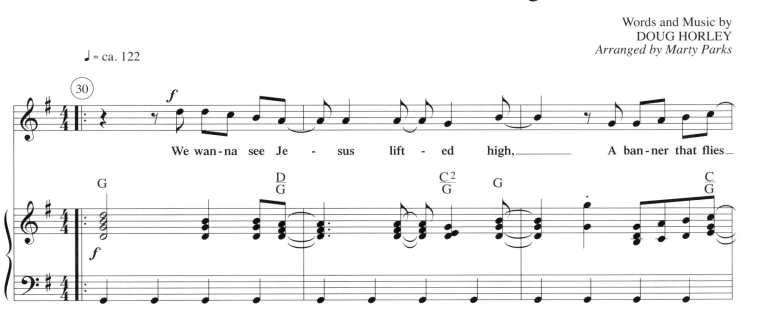

Song begins on page 8 in the Choral Edition

HIGH AND LIFTED UP

includes
Salvation Belongs to Our God
I See the Lord
Step by Step

Medley arranged by Marty Parks

Presentation Suggestions:
   SALVATION BELONGS TO OUR GOD: Verse 1, 1st ending; Verse 2, medley ending
   I SEE THE LORD: One time, medley ending
   STEP BY STEP: Repeat ending, medley ending

Salvation Belongs to Our God

Words and Music by
ADRIAN HOWARD
and PAT TURNER
Arranged by Marty Parks

I See the Lord

Words and Music by
CHRIS FALSON
Arranged by Marty Parks

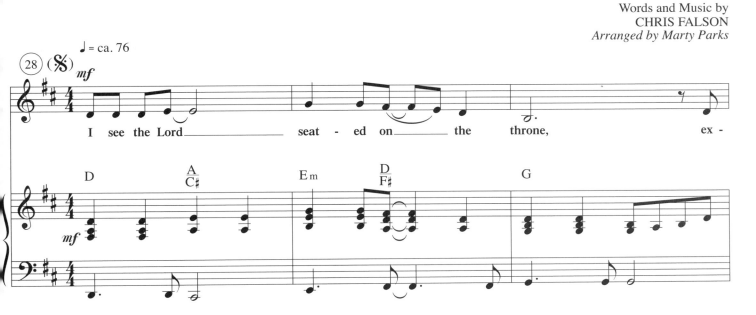

14

Step by Step

Words and Music by
DAVID STRASSER
Arranged by Marty Parks

18

Song begins on page 14 in the Choral Edition

BOW IN WORSHIP

includes
Ancient of Days
Come, Now Is the Time to Worship

Medley arranged by Marty Parks

Presentation Suggestions:
ANCIENT OF DAYS: 1st ending, 2nd ending, medley ending
COME, NOW IS THE TIME TO WORSHIP: 1 time, medley ending

Ancient of Days

Words and Music by
JAMIE HARVILL
and GARY SADLER
Arranged by Marty Parks

Bless - ing_____ and hon - or, glo - ry_____ and pow - er

Ev - 'ry knee____ shall bow at Your throne_____ in wor - ship;

You will be____ ex - alt - ed, O God, and Your

king - dom____ shall not pass a - way,_____ O An - cient of Days.

CD 1:22 / 24 1st / 2nd time

1

(to pg. 18, meas. 5)

22

Come, Now Is the Time to Worship

Words and Music by
BRIAN DOERKSEN
Arranged by Marty Parks

just as you are _____ to wor - - ship; _____

D $\frac{G}{D}$ D $\frac{G}{D}$ D

Come,   just   as   you   are _____ be -

A $\frac{Em}{A}$ A^6 A

fore   your   God;   come.

Em   Bm   A   D

CD 1:27

One   day   ev - 'ry   tongue   will   con - fess _____

D $\frac{D}{F\sharp}$ $\frac{D}{A}$ G   D

CD 1:29

Song begins on page 23 in the Choral Edition

HOLINESS

includes
More than Worthy
Take My Life

Medley arranged by Marty Parks

Presentation Suggestions:
MORE THAN WORTHY: 1st ending, 2nd ending, medley ending
TAKE MY LIFE: 1st ending, 2nd ending, 3rd ending

More than Worthy

Words and Music by
CHRISTINE HAYS
Arranged by Marty Parks

I wor - ship You with sing - ing, _____ I

wor - ship You with all of my heart; _____ I wor - ship You, I

Song ending

can - not be si - lent, Lord, I will praise _____ Your _____ name.

Medley ending

Lord, I will praise _____ Your _____ name.

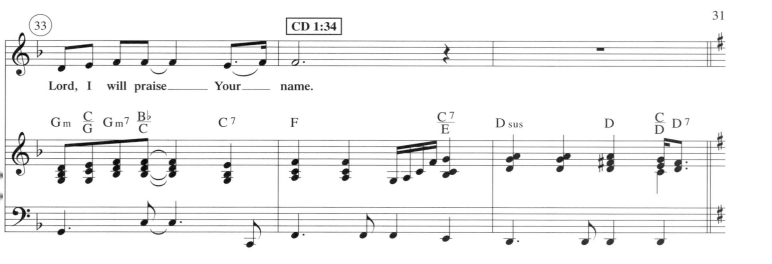

Take My Life

Words and Music by
SCOTT UNDERWOOD
Arranged by Marty Parks

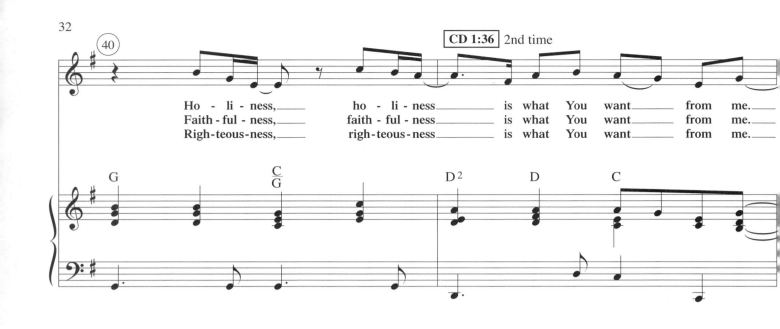

Ho - li - ness,_____ ho - li - ness_____ is what You want_____ from me.
Faith - ful - ness,_____ faith - ful - ness_____ is what You want_____ from me.
Righ - teous - ness,_____ righ-teous - ness_____ is what You want_____ from me.

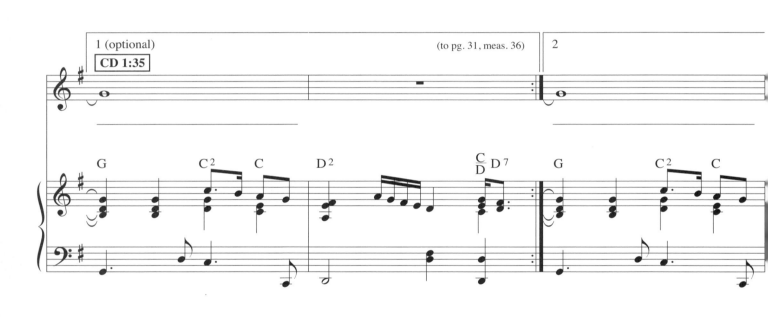

1 (optional)   (to pg. 31, meas. 36)   2

So take my heart,_____ and form

Song begins on page 28 in the Choral Edition

Because We Believe

Words and Music by
JAMIE HARVILL
and NANCY GORDON
Arranged by Marty Parks

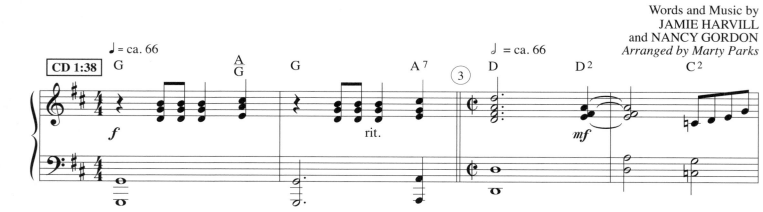

42

Song begins on page 35 in the Choral Edition

YOU ARE MY LIFE

includes
Jesus, You Are My Life
Knowing You
Let My Words Be Few

Medley arranged by Marty Parks

Presentation Suggestions:
    JESUS, YOU ARE MY LIFE: Verse 1, repeat ending; Verse 3, medley ending
    KNOWING YOU: Verse 1; Refrain, repeat ending; Verse 2; Refrain, medley ending
    LET MY WORDS BE FEW: Repeat ending, medley ending

Jesus, You Are My Life

Words and Music by
STEVE FRY
Arranged by Marty Parks

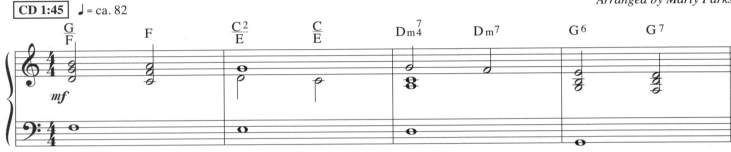

(to pg. 42, meas. 5)

Song ending

life.

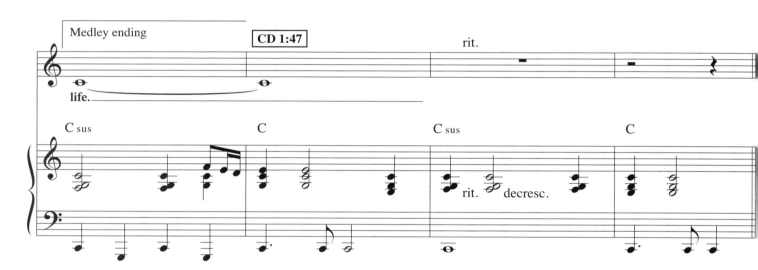

Medley ending

CD 1:47

rit.

life.

Knowing You

Words and Music by
GRAHAM KENDRICK
Arranged by Marty Parks

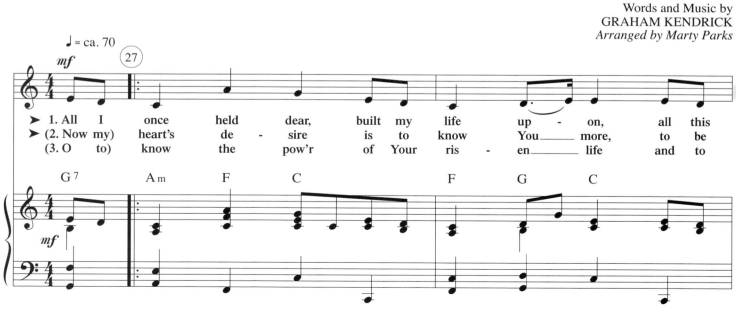

♩ = ca. 70

mf

27

➤ 1. All I once held dear, built my life up - on, all this
➤ (2. Now my) heart's de - sire is to know You____ more, to be
(3. O to) know the pow'r of Your ris - en____ life and to

Let My Words Be Few

BETH REDMAN

MATT REDMAN
Arranged by Marty Parks

Song begins on page 40 in the Choral Edition

I NEED YOU

includes

I Need You More
Breathe on Me
The Heart of Worship

Medley arranged by Marty Parks

Presentation Suggestions:
I NEED YOU MORE: One time with D.S., Coda, medley ending
BREATHE ON ME: Verse 1, medley ending
THE HEART OF WORSHIP: Verse 1, D.S. repeat ending, medley ending

I Need You More

Words and Music by
LINDELL COOLEY
and BRUCE HAYNES
Arranged by Marty Parks

Breathe on Me

Words and Music by
LUCY FISHER
Arranged by Marty Parks

The Heart of Worship

Words and Music by
MATT REDMAN
Arranged by Marty Parks

(to pg. 55, meas. 65)

D.S. repeat ending

D.S.
(to pg. 57, meas. 81)

all a-bout You,___ Je - sus.

E♭   E♭sus   A♭M⁷   B♭6   B♭7

Song ending

Medley ending

all a-bout You,___ Je - sus._____

all a-bout You,___ Je - sus.

A♭M⁷   B♭6   B♭7   E♭

A♭M⁷   B♭6   B♭7   E♭

decresc.

97   mf

I'll bring You more than a song,___

E♭   E♭sus   E♭/G   Fm⁷   E♭/G

decresc.   mf

rit.   mp

Je - sus._____

B♭sus   B♭   E♭   E♭2

rit.   mp

Song begins on page 48 in the Choral Edition

MY REFUGE

includes

You, O Lord, Are My Refuge
Better Is One Day

Medley arranged by Marty Parks

Presentation Suggestions:
YOU, O LORD, ARE MY REFUGE: 2nd ending; D.S., medley ending
BETTER IS ONE DAY: Verse 1, 1st ending; Verse 2, 2nd ending; Refrain, 1st ending;
Verse 3, 3rd ending; Refrain, 2nd ending; D.S., refrain, medley ending

You, O Lord, Are My Refuge

Words and Music by
CHERI KEAGGY
Arranged by Marty Parks

Better Is One Day

Words and Music by
MATT REDMAN
Arranged by Marty Parks

Song begins on page 54 in the Choral Edition

MY KING

includes
Above All
You Are My King
You Are My All in All

Medley arranged by Marty Parks

Presentation Suggestions:
  ABOVE ALL: Repeat ending, medley ending
  YOU ARE MY KING: Medley ending
  YOU ARE MY ALL IN ALL: Verse 1; Refrain, medley ending; Verse 2; Refrain, medley
    ending

Above All

Words and Music by
LENNY LEBLANC
and PAUL BALOCHE
Arranged by Marty Parks

68

You Are My King

Words and Music by
BILLY JAMES FOOTE
Arranged by Marty Park

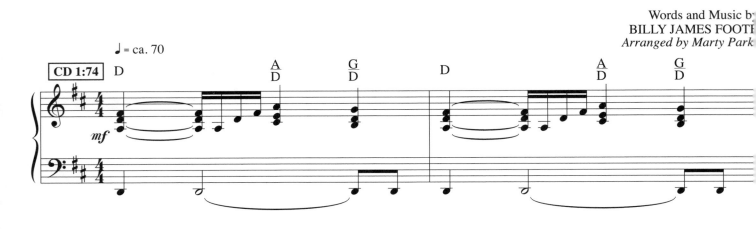

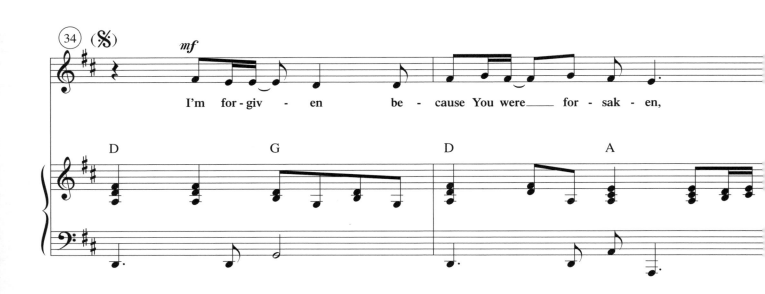

I'm for-giv-en be-cause You were for-sak-en,

I'm ac-cept-ed, You were con-demned.

You Are My All in All

Words and Music by
DENNIS JERNIGAN
Arranged by Marty Park

76

Song begins on page 64 in the Choral Edition

WE GATHER IN YOUR PRESENCE

includes
As We Gather
We Thank You for Your Presence

Medley arranged by Marty Parks

Presentation Suggestions:
AS WE GATHER: Repeat ending, medley ending
WE THANK YOU FOR YOUR PRESENCE: D.S., repeat ending, medley ending

As We Gather

Words and Music by
MIKE FAY and TOM COOMES
Arranged by Marty Parks

Medley Sequence copyright © 2001 by PsalmSinger Music (BMI). All rights reserved.
Administered by The Copyright Company, 40 Music Square East, Nashville, TN 37203.

PLEASE NOTE: Copying of this product is NOT covered by CCLI licenses. For CCLI information call 1-800-234-2446.

We Thank You for Your Presence

Words and Music by
MARTIN NYSTROM
Arranged by Marty Parks

Wher - ev - er two___ or more___ have gath-ered in___ Your name,___ Your

pres - ence,___ O Lord,___ will be there in that place.___ So we

have - n't an - y doubt___ You're here a-mong___ us now,___

Song begins on page 70 in the Choral Edition

CELEBRATE!

includes
I Will Celebrate (Duvall)
I Will Celebrate (Baloche)

Medley arranged by Marty Parks

Presentation Suggestions:
I WILL CELEBRATE (Duvall): One time, medley ending
I WILL CELEBRATE (Baloche): One time

I Will Celebrate

Words and Music by
LINDA DUVALL
Arranged by Marty Parks

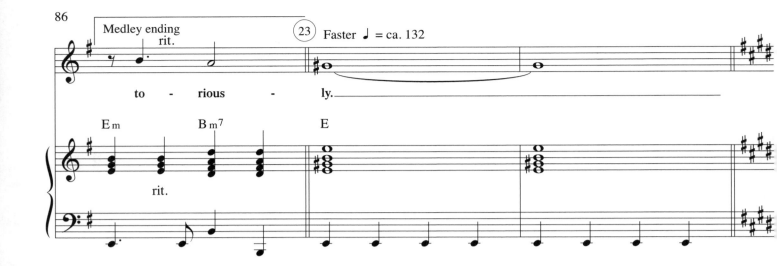

I Will Celebrate

Words and Music by
RITA BALOCHE
Arranged by Marty Parks

CD 2:5

Song begins on page 76 in the Choral Edition

CROWNED WITH PRAISE

includes
We Fall Down
You Are Crowned with Praise
Blessing, Honor, and Glory

Medley arranged by Marty Parks

Presentation Suggestions:
WE FALL DOWN: Repeat ending, medley ending
YOU ARE CROWNED WITH PRAISE: Medley ending
BLESSING, HONOR, AND GLORY: 1st ending, 2nd ending

We Fall Down

Words and Music by
CHRIS TOMLIN
Arranged by Marty Parks

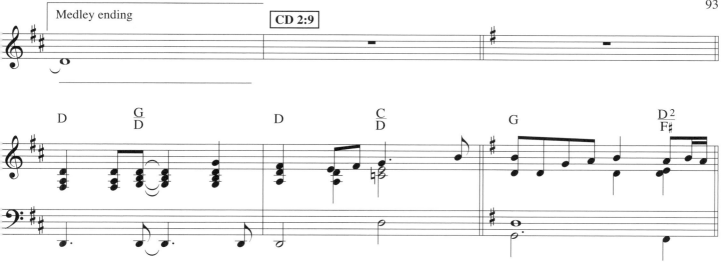

You Are Crowned with Praise

Words and Music by
CHRISTY COOPER
Arranged by Marty Parks

94

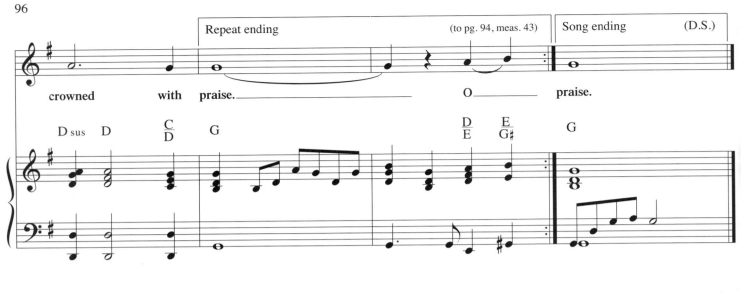

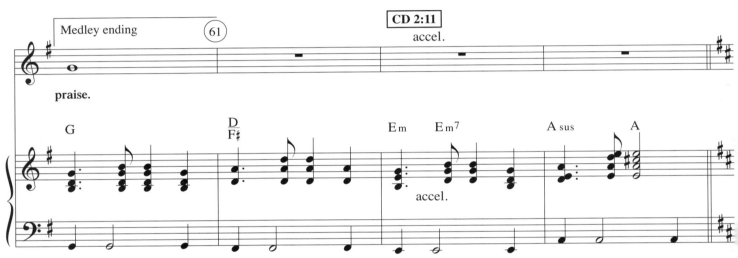

Blessing, Honor, and Glory

Words and Music by
GEOFF BULLOCK
and DAVID REIDY
Arranged by Marty Parks

(to pg. 97, meas. 72)

Song begins on page 83 in the Choral Edition

HOLY OF HOLIES

includes

Jesus, Draw Me Close
When I Look into Your Holiness
Come into the Holy of Holies

Medley arranged by Marty Parks

Presentation Suggestions:
 JESUS, DRAW ME CLOSE: One time, medley ending
 WHEN I LOOK INTO YOUR HOLINESS: Repeat ending, medley ending
 COME INTO THE HOLY OF HOLIES: Medley ending

Jesus, Draw Me Close

Words and Music by
RICK FOUNDS
Arranged by Marty Parks

When I Look into Your Holiness

Words and Music by
WAYNE and CATHY PERRIN
Arranged by Marty Parks

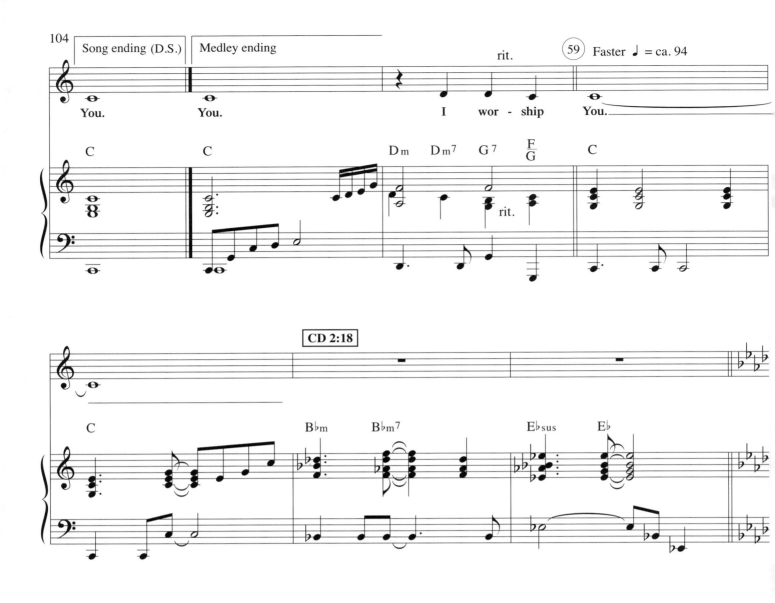

Come into the Holy of Holies

Words and Music by
JOHN SELLERS
Arranged by Marty Parks

Song begins on page 91 in the Choral Edition

I WANT TO SEE YOU

includes
Open Our Eyes, Lord
Open the Eyes of My Heart

Medley arranged by Marty Parks

Presentation Suggestions:
OPEN OUR EYES, LORD: One time, medley ending
OPEN THE EYES OF MY HEART: With repeats

Open Our Eyes, Lord

Words and Music by
ROBERT CULL
Arranged by Marty Parks

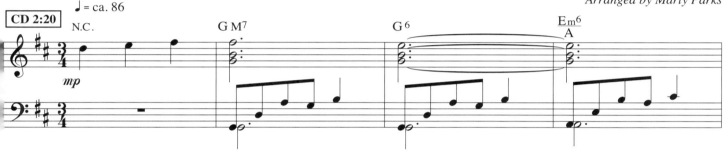

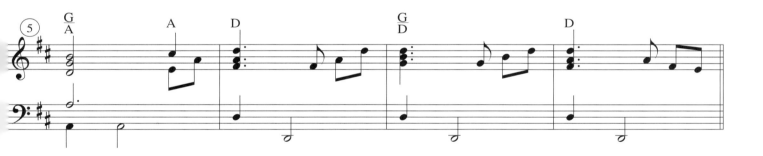

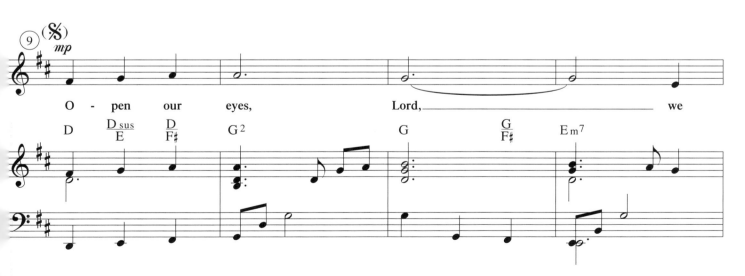

110

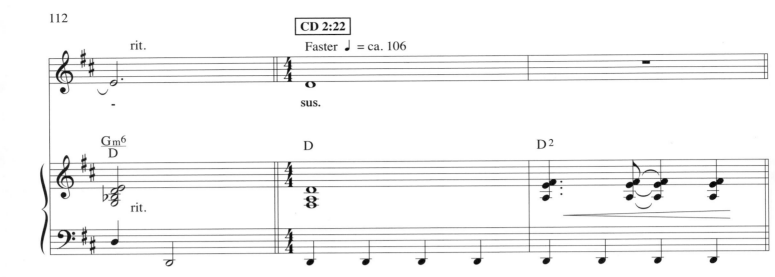

Open the Eyes of My Heart

Words and Music by
PAUL BALOCHE
Arranged by Marty Parks

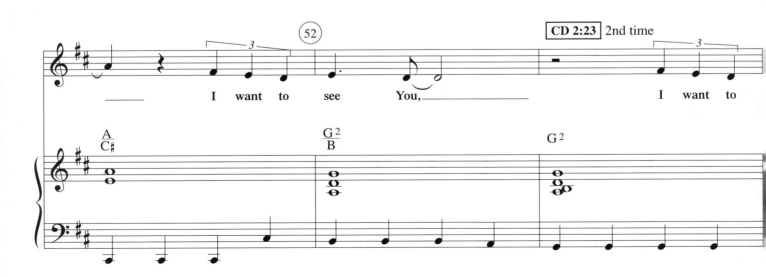

Song begins on page 97 in the Choral Edition

AWESOME AND HOLY

includes

Holy, You Are Holy
Awesome in This Place
Be Magnified

Medley arranged by Marty Parks

Presentation Suggestions:
  HOLY, YOU ARE HOLY: Repeat ending, medley ending
  AWESOME IN THIS PLACE: repeat ending; D.S. repeat ending; Medley ending
  BE MAGNIFIED: One time, medley ending, medley ending

Holy, You Are Holy

Words and Music by
BRUCE WICKERSHEIM
Arranged by Marty Parks

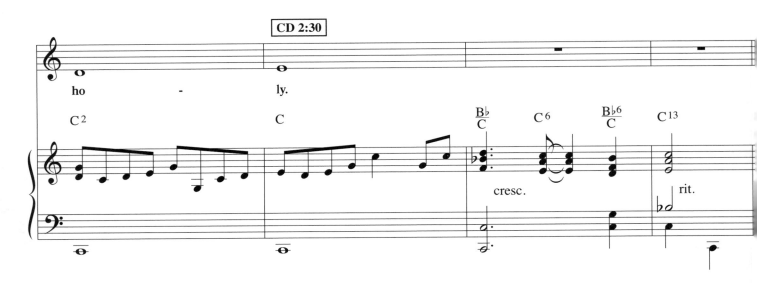

Awesome in This Place

Words and Music by
DAVE BILLINGTON
Arranged by Marty Parks

Be Magnified

Words and Music by
LYNN DESHAZO
Arranged by Marty Parks

122

Song begins on page 105 in the Choral Edition

YOUR LOVE SURROUNDS ME

includes
Desire of My Heart
The Power of Your Love
I Could Sing of Your Love Forever

Medley arranged by Marty Parks

Presentation Suggestions:
DESIRE OF MY HEART: One time, medley ending
THE POWER OF YOUR LOVE: Verse 1, repeat ending; Verse 2, medley ending
I COULD SING OF YOUR LOVE FOREVER: One time, medley ending

Desire of My Heart

Words and Music by
MARTY PARKS
Arranged by Marty Parks

Repeat ending   (to pg. 124, meas. 5)

O De - sire of my heart.

Gm7   C7   F

Song ending   Medley ending

heart.   heart.

F   F2   F   F/A

25

O De - sire of my heart.   O De - sire of my

C7   F   F/A   C7   Dm/C C7 Dm/C   C

rit.

heart;   my   heart.

F   F/E♭   D sus   D7

rit.

The Power of Your Love

Words and Music by
GEOFF BULLOCK
Arranged by Marty Parks

128

130

I Could Sing of Your Love Forever

Words and Music by
MARTIN SMITH
Arranged by Marty Parks

Song begins on page 113 in the Choral Edition

SONG OF TRUST

includes
He Is Able
Ever Faithful
God Is the Strength of My Heart

Medley arranged by Marty Park

Presentation Suggestions:
  HE IS ABLE: One time, medley ending
  EVER FAITHFUL: Repeat ending, medley ending
  GOD IS THE STRENGTH OF MY HEART: One time, medley ending

He Is Able

Words and Music by
RORY NOLAND and
GREG FERGUSON
Arranged by Marty Park

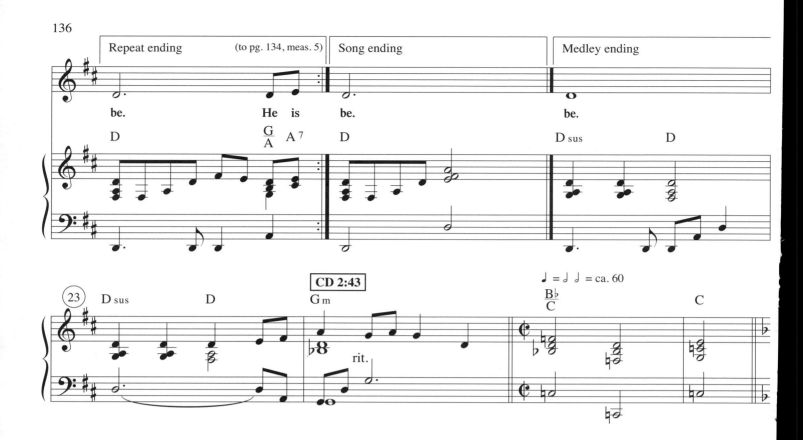

Ever Faithful

Words and Music by
BRUCE WICKERSHEIM
Arranged by Marty Parks

139

God Is the Strength of My Heart

Words and Music by
EUGENE GRECO
Arranged by Marty Parks

144

Song begins on page 122 in the Choral Edition

WE WORSHIP YOU

includes

To Worship You
There Is None like You
I Worship You, Almighty God

Medley arranged by Marty Parks

Presentation Suggestions:
TO WORSHIP YOU: Verse 1, medley ending
THERE IS NONE LIKE YOU: With repeats as written, medley ending
I WORSHIP YOU, ALMIGHTY GOD: One time, medley ending

To Worship You

EN BIBLE

TOM FETTKE and
RICHARD KINGSMORE
Arranged by Marty Parks

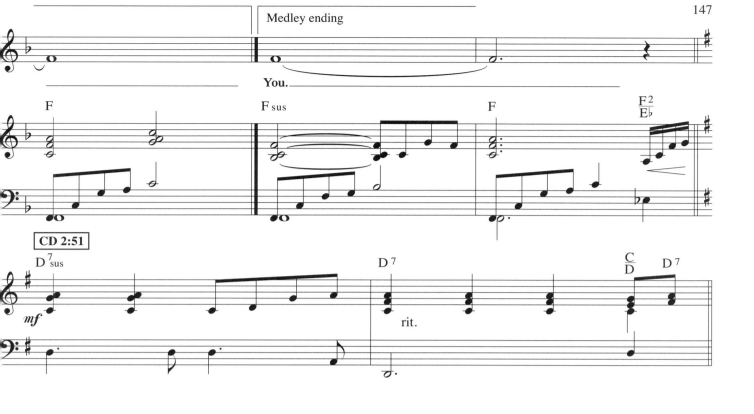

There Is None like You

Words and Music by
LENNY LEBLANC
Arranged by Marty Parks

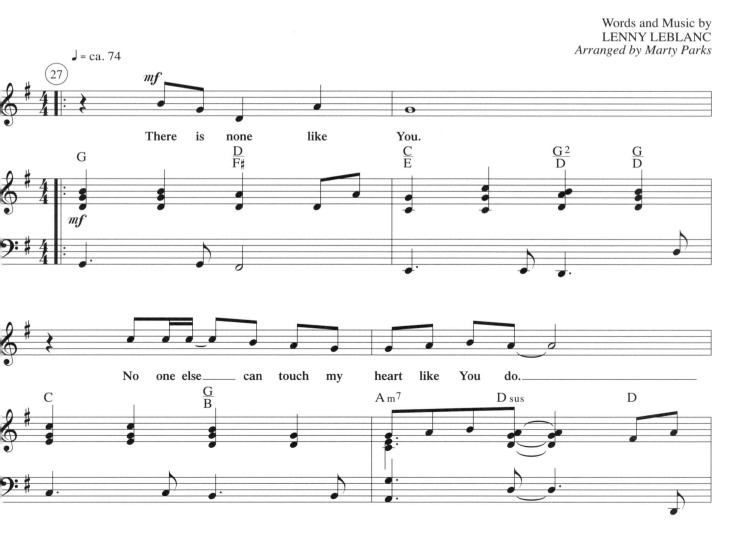

(to pg. 147, meas. 27)

I Worship You, Almighty God

Words and Music by
SONDRA CORBETT WOOD
Arranged by Marty Parks

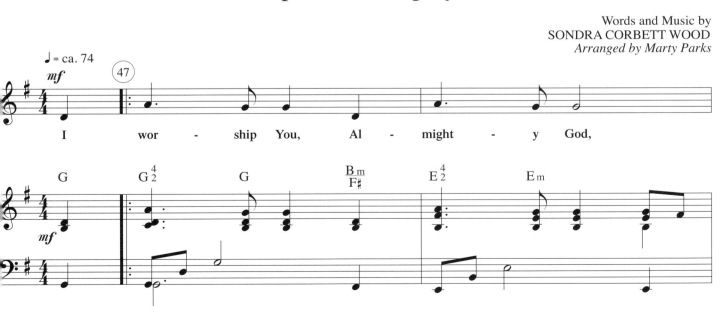

Song begins on page 128 in the Choral Edition

YOU ARE THE POTTER

includes

Change My Heart, O God
I Will Never Be the Same
The Potter's Hand

Medley arranged by Marty Parks

Presentation Suggestions:
    CHANGE MY HEART, O GOD: One time with D.S, medley ending
    I WILL NEVER BE THE SAME: One time, medley ending
    THE POTTER'S HAND: Repeat ending, medley ending

Change My Heart, O God

Words and Music by
EDDIE ESPINOSA
Arranged by Marty Parks

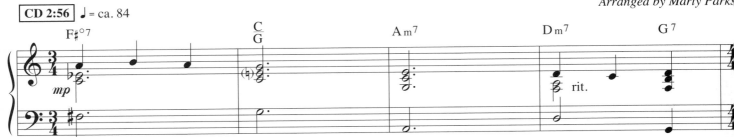

Medley Sequence copyright © 2001 by PsalmSinger Music (BMI). All rights reserved.
Administered by The Copyright Company, 40 Music Square East, Nashville, TN 37203.

PLEASE NOTE: Copying of this product is NOT covered by CCLI licenses. For CCLI information call 1-800-234-2446.

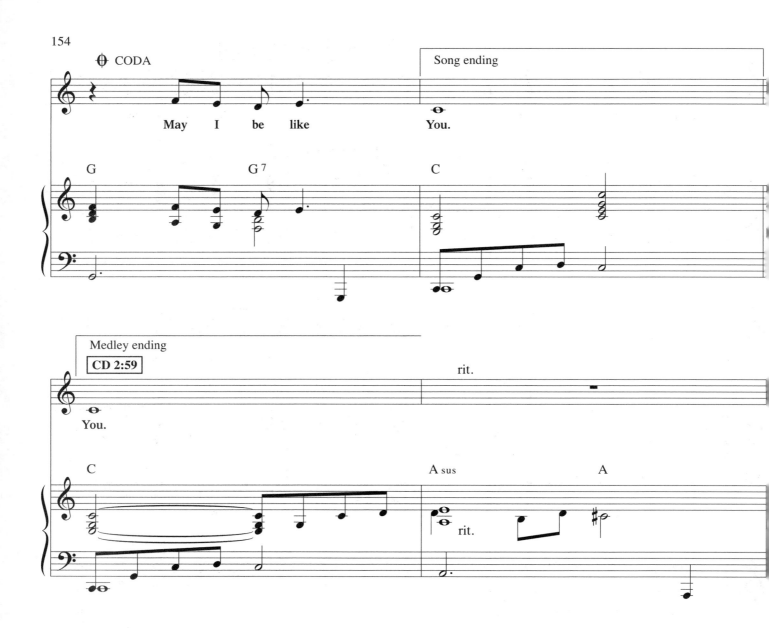

CODA

Song ending

May I be like You.

Medley ending

CD 2:59

You.

rit.

I Will Never Be the Same

Words and Music by
GEOFF BULLOCK
Arranged by Marty Parks

♩ = ca. 78

mf

I will nev-er be the same a - gain;

The Potter's Hand

Words and Music by
DARLENE ZSCHECH
Arranged by Marty Park

Song begins on page 136 in the Choral Edition

LAMB OF GOD

includes

Agnus Dei

Hallelujah to the Lamb

Medley arranged by Marty Park

Presentation Suggestions:
AGNUS DEI: 1st & 2nd endings, repeat ending, medley ending
HALLELUJAH TO THE LAMB: Verse 1; Refrain, 1st ending; Verse 2; Refrain, 2nd ending, medley ending

Agnus Dei

Words and Music by
MICHAEL W. SMITH
Arranged by Marty Park

Hallelujah to the Lamb

Words and Music b
DON MOEN an
DEBBYE GRAAFSM
Arranged by Marty Park

168

glo - ry, giv-ing hon - or, giv-ing praise un - to the Lamb____ of God.____

Ev - 'ry knee shall bow,____

ev - 'ry tongue con - fess that You are Lord of All!____

ALPHABETICAL INDEX

Song and Medley Titles

Individual medley orchestrations available upon request.